A MEMOIR

DJ BAD THA PROBLEM

For permission requests, contact the publisher at the website below:

CERTIFIED HITz Music Group

Website: https://www.certifiedhitzmusicgroup.com/

Photographs provided by CERTIFIED HITz Music Group

Printed in the United States of America

ISBN: 979-8-218-71384-3

eBook ISBN: 979-8-218-68031-2

This is a memoir and a work of nonfiction. The events, people, and places described are based on the author's personal experiences and memories. Some names and identifying details may have been changed to protect privacy, but any resemblance to actual persons, living or dead, or real events is intentional and reflects the author's life story.

Dedicated to Jaq, Barbara
and to the old me

The realest shit I ever wrote, I told my mom I will never go broke. Never slip up, never choke.

— DJ Bad Tha Problem

PREFACE

I know what some of y'all may be thinking…

GROUP CHAT

Who the hell is DJ BAD THA PROBLEM?

Why are you writing a book?!

What makes you so special?

I never heard of you. You're not even famous what are you writing a book for? Lol!

DJ BAD THA PROBLEM

Well, I'm glad you asked…

See, I'm just a young kid from New Jersey with a dream who is very ambitious. Growing up, I didn't realize how ambitious I was. In fact, it didn't occur to me until I was in my early twenties.

Anyway, my dream was to make it in the music business. Why? Because I am very passionate about music and music production. I couldn't care less about the fame. People who know me well know I hate being the center of attention. The money? I mean, money is cool and all. But let's be honest… If I were in it for the money, I would have called it quits a long time ago. I mean, think about it... Anybody who is only concerned with making money, especially fast money. We all know that these particular individuals are not gonna last long. Right? Because they are going to realize that the business just doesn't work like that. Life in general doesn't work like that. And if that's all you care about?? Well, you're in it for the wrong reasons. Mind you, I have been doing music for well over a decade now.

I didn't start seeing real success or money till my mid to late twenties. Through the years, I have single-handedly taken care of everything, a practice that persists to the present. Well... some stuff anyway. At the time, I was broke and couldn't afford to pay anybody to do the things that I needed help with. However, that is not to say I didn't have help along the way, as you'll find out when you read this book.

I give credit where credit is due. I'm not one of those people who act like they did everything by themselves and take all the credit. When these people know, deep down, they **clearly** had help. But for whatever reason, they don't want to admit it. If you're that type of person reading this.

You know you're wrong, stop being so damn selfish and change your ways.

Let me stop ranting...

Anyway, why did I write this book? You see, I had two very close friends of mine, Jaq and Barbara. Jaq, I have known since high school, and Barbara was not only a close friend but a second mom to me. They knew how passionate I was about music and breaking into the industry. When something exciting happened. I would be the first to tell them.

I remember when I started to see a little sprout of success from doing mixtapes. Both of them suggested I should write a book about my story and how I was able to accomplish the things that I'd accomplished over the years. But at the time, I felt like it was too early and I didn't really accomplish anything.

But now looking back, I realize the time is right. I've done a lot and it's time to talk about it. So, why not tell my story? I may not be famous… **Yet**. But mark my words.

You will hear about me. *I guarantee it.*

My two close friends that I mentioned earlier passed away years ago. But I know they are up in heaven looking down and smiling from ear to ear because they have seen how far I've come and the struggles I went through both mentally and physically. That's why I am writing this book. This book is dedicated to them. I made a promise, and this is me keeping and following through on that promise.

I love y'all and miss y'all every day Jaq and Barbara. This is for you. I know I am making you both proud. I wish you were here to witness it. Thank you for believing in me and never giving up on me.

Now, I'm sure you're wondering why I also dedicated this book to the "old me." Back when I was a kid, even in my pre-teen to teenage years, I was very weak-minded. When I would tell people about my dreams, they would laugh in my face and tell me.

"You will never make it."

"That's impossible."

"Yeah, okay buddy."

You name it. I'm pretty sure you've heard similar sayings before. Even my parents didn't believe in me. Of course, they think differently now.

Being a kid with highly ambitious goals and hearing people laugh and stomp all over your dreams really affects your confidence. During that time, I wanted to give up. I started to think maybe my parents, family members, and friends were right. But then, as I got older... I realized that all they were doing was projecting their insecurities onto me. Plus, I know that when I put my mind to something that I am passionate about and actively work at it each day, it's hard for me to stop. So to the old me... or should I say the younger me.

> Look at us... We did it!! You manifested a dream, you put in the work. It took a long time but the hard work is paying off. You're starting to see the fruits of your labor. Do not let anybody try to downplay your accomplishments.

With that being said, for those of you who laugh at the idea of me writing a book just because I'm not famous, or special and nobody cares about my story. Just know that...

I don't give a fuck!!
Now sit back, relax, and watch me work.
I got hitz for days and a story to tell.

CONTENTS

CHAPTER 1
THE PRELUDE

Allow me to reintroduce myself. My name is Eli. I was born and raised in New Jersey, also known as the Garden State. Since my early childhood, I've actively sought out and enjoyed a wide variety of musical genres, dedicating myself to fully experiencing each one.

In school, I was a curious and observant child with an overwhelming desire to learn music theory and master a diverse range of musical instruments. This consumed a lot of my time in music class. Struggling, I found myself wrestling with the complexities of both. Yet I continued to push forward in my efforts to gain expertise in each.

I even learned how to play the clarinet... sort of. But reading music? Still can't do that. Even to this day, I still don't know how. That's why, when it comes to making beats or producing, I just play it by ear.

My initial plans changed however, as I subsequently recognized a deeper fascination with music production. Fueling a stronger interest in pursuing further education and training in this field. Throughout my upbringing, our home and car rides were filled with the sounds of different types of music, courtesy of my parents. From Rap, Hip Hop, Jazz to Oldies. Music has always been a part of my life. While listening to music, I've always analyzed not only the song and instrumental, but how the record overall was mixed and thought to myself…

"How did they do that?!"

"What program did they use to record this song?"

"What sounds were used to make this beat??"

This early exposure sparked my deep love for the art form and because of my curious mind, I wanted to learn more.

It wasn't until I turned sixteen that my journey into music truly began. One late evening while flipping through television channels, I stumbled upon a documentary shown on B.E.T. about Hip Hop and the music industry. The documentary featured some of the most iconic figures in the industry: Kanye West, DJ Scratch, DJ Drama, and Dr. Dre. Each legend shared their unique stories and contributions, painting a vivid picture of a world I had only dreamed of.

Watching those Hip Hop legends, I felt something click. "I wanted to learn how to do it all." Not just rap or make beats. I wanted the whole playbook. The documentary was more than just a film; it was a revelation that ignited a fire within me. Awakening a passion not just for music but for the entire creative process behind it.

 I wanted to learn how to do it all.

ELI

THE PRELUDE

That Christmas, my dream began to take shape. Recognizing my newfound passion, my family came together to gift me a modest collection of studio equipment. It was only the beginning for me. With just a basic setup and a hunger to learn, I turned a corner of my bedroom into a home studio.

Every day after school, I would rush home eager to dive into the art of music production. I spent hours reading books on audio engineering, learning the ins and outs of each piece of equipment, digital audio workstation, and overall sharpening my skills. It wasn't just a hobby; it was a constant pursuit of perfecting my craft. My dedication to mastering the craft was firm, driven by a desire to create something meaningful and impactful.

This was only the beginning...

CHAPTER 2
MASTERING THE ARTS

When I turned eighteen, my family came through again. This time with a set of CDJs and a mixer. That gift marked a whole new chapter for me. At first, I wanted to rap. But eventually, I realized my real passion was behind the decks. That's when I shifted from trying to be an artist to a DJ. My fascination with the art of DJing grew as I delved into the world of mixing different genres of music and learning different skill sets.

I devoured every piece of information I could find, from YouTube tutorials to DJ forums. I practiced tirelessly, experimenting with different genres, techniques, and soon began to develop my unique style. The excitement of blending tracks, creating seamless transitions, and crafting new mixes was thrilling.

With a desire to expand my reach and share my latest mixes to a wider range of listeners, I began actively uploading my work to several online platforms, including popular sites like Myspace and SoundCloud. While my early mixes were unpolished and perhaps a bit rough around the edges, they carried a spark that caught the attention of those who heard them. The response was mostly positive, and my mixes started to gain traction. The growing number of friend requests and feedback on both Myspace and SoundCloud were early signs that my mixes were resonating with other people. Sure, I got some hate too. But I never let it shake me. I stayed locked in, focused, and remained dedicated to my craft. After all, most of us weren't born naturally gifted. I understood early on that some people wouldn't be a fan of me or my work, and that's okay. Besides… I wasn't gonna let any negativity I received deter me from accomplishing my dreams.

> *Side note: I'm going to be honest. Looking back on the mixes I've created many years later and comparing them to my latest material now. They were not very good. A night and day difference, if we're strictly talking about quality. My old mixes were not "Certified Hitz", as I like to say. More like, "Certified Cheeks". And no, I'm not referring to the ones on your face either.*

That's when I adopted the name **DJ BAD THA PROBLEM**, a nickname my homegirl Jaq gave me back in high school. It was bold, raw, and unapologetic. Just like me. By choosing this name, I was making a powerful statement about my ambition to transform the music industry. Signaling my preparedness to meet and take on any challenges I encountered in chasing my dream.

My first year of DJing, I started working with various unsigned artists whom I'd met through the social media platform Myspace. These collaborations were more than just your typical collabs; they were opportunities to learn and grow. Together, we created mixtapes with the shared goal of breaking into the industry and hopefully securing deals with major labels.

I was all in on helping unsigned artists, and this led to me joining **Purple Label Ent.**, an independent label where I worked alongside rapper 45 Tha Feva. The experience was invaluable, providing me with insights into the ins and outs of the music industry and the challenges faced by aspiring artists. It was a period of immense growth.

As DJ BAD THA PROBLEM, I was determined to leave my mark. Not just by learning and mastering the craft of music and music production. But by mastering and dominating the business.

CHAPTER 3
THE GRIND AND THE GLOW UP

As music and the industry evolved, I shifted from Myspace to Twitter. I adapted swiftly, using the platform to network, push artists, and get my mixtapes heard.

The grind started paying off when I linked up with DJ Kelo, the founder of *Team Titan DJs*. DJ Kelo, recognizing my talent and determination, became a mentor and an important figure in my career.

DJ Kelo's mentorship opened new doors and provided valuable information about the music industry. With his guidance, my network expanded, and I began to connect with other influential figures in music. This connection led me to join *Team Titan DJs*, a collective of talented DJs known for their love of music, high-level skills, and dedication to the art of DJing.

With Team Titan DJs, my journey took a significant turn and a newfound hunger erupted inside of me. Week after week, I consistently released mixtapes for two years straight. Flooding the internet with new music. No breaks. Just work. The grind was real—but I embraced it. Not only did I demonstrate a powerful work ethic, but

I also thrived in the demanding and competitive environment. A fact that was clearly recognized and appreciated by others.

As more time went by, it dawned on me that building a strong team was crucial for my success. Specifically for marketing and promotion. For many years, I was doing all the heavy lifting by myself. From the mixing, mastering, graphic design, marketing, and promotion. While fully self-sufficient and more than capable of handling tasks independently, I had no reservations about working alone. However, I eventually realized I couldn't keep doing everything solo. Even the biggest artists have teams and I needed one too.

Furthermore, it is important to remember that there will always be individuals who surpass you in terms of skill and experience. We all have our strengths and weaknesses. That's why building a team was crucial. Taking everything into consideration, I started my search.

 Furthermore, it is important to remember that there will always be individuals who surpass you in terms of skill and experience.

Through a mutual friend and business partner, I connected with Johnathan, also known as GD. A young entrepreneur fresh out of high school. At the time, I was looking for people to join my marketing and promotion team and thought Johnathan would be a good fit. Johnathan told me that he wasn't too knowledgeable about the music business and how it works, but he was willing to learn and hustle. That was enough for me.

I laid out simple instructions about what I needed him to do, and Johnathan went to work promoting my newly released material. Whether it was mash-ups, mixes, or mixtapes. Within a short period of working together, Johnathan came across a group of marketers and promoters who were interested in my work. He told them what he was doing for me, and they agreed to help him further. Thanks to

Johnathan and the group of marketers and promoters, things rapidly began to change.

Suddenly, my mixtapes and mashups started catching fire, becoming incredibly popular and attracting a lot of attention. Gaining hundreds of thousands of streams monthly.[i] My social media following increased. My mixtapes were being bootlegged and sold on different websites, such as eBay.[ii] They were even being sold internationally.[iii] Not only did my fan base grow domestically, but my exceptional work also gained worldwide recognition, resulting in an ever-growing international fan base that still surprises me today.

The internet buzzed with anticipation for each new release, and my reputation as a mixtape DJ grew. My varied mixes drawing from multiple genres found a broad audience. The mixtapes success not only captured the attention of a growing fan base but also that of industry professionals, thus creating opportunities that had previously seemed unattainable.

This success led to an exciting new venture, radio. I began hosting my own show titled *"Tha Problem Hour"* on **Da Grind Music Radio**, an internet radio station. The show expanded my reach and introduced me to a bigger audience. My journey continued to gain momentum daily, and this was yet another significant achievement in a progression that seemed to accelerate with every passing day.

I later connected with DJ Pop Dukez, the founder of **24K Mixtape DJs**. He'd heard about me and my work through his business partner Derrick.

Even though he was hesitant to let me join at first, Pop enlisted me as a member of his DJ crew after being persuaded by his fellow business partner. Through his efforts in creating and organizing opportunities, he significantly expanded my professional network and helped me connect with numerous individuals.

Even with my incredible run, I remained grounded. I remembered my start in New Jersey and the passion that had driven me from the start. The journey had been one of trials and tribulations, but each challenge had only served to strengthen my determination.

CHAPTER 4
BREAKING BARRIERS AND MAKING NOISE

With a firm footing, I began to expand my horizons. My reputation as a mixtape DJ opened doors to collaborations with various major artists in the industry, including Short Dawg and many others.[i,ii]

These weren't just wins on paper, they meant everything. It showed how far I'd come and how much further I could go. Exceeding the sum of my initial expectations.

Besides producing mixtapes, I ventured into artist management and development. I always used to tell myself that I didn't want to be categorized or put into a box by others, preferring to maintain my versatility. I've always had a hustler's mentality. It's difficult to say for certain where this came from, but I suspect it was a gift from my pops. This mindset birthed, BAD the *entrepreneur*.

I took on the role of not just being a DJ, but an A&R, helping up-and-coming artists navigate the complexities of the music industry. My passion for nurturing new talent led to the establishment of *CERTIFIED HITz Music Group*, an independent record label dedicated to promoting and supporting emerging artists. One of my most notable and frequent collaborators is with an artist whom I've been working with for fifteen years, City The Great. Together, we released numerous mixtapes over time. Each mixtape we released garnered not only an abundance of streams but also legendary attention.

Thanks to City's undeniable talent and help from one of his long-time friends, City The Great is currently being mentored by Hip-Hop legends Special Ed and Kool Rock Ski of **The Fat Boys.**[iii] It's clear that our partnership was a success and continues to be successful, and it solidified my reputation as one of the key people in his career.

My second most notable and frequent collaborator is Poka Jones, a rising independent Southern Soul artist from Atlanta. My support for Poka extended beyond marketing and promotion. I helped him by offering guidance and making important business decisions regarding his career. Together, we released a mixtape titled *"The Best of Poka Jones."* The mixtape was released on all streaming platforms back in February of 2021 and has now accumulated over half a million streams.

When I saw my mixtape catalog pass 4.1 million streams, I was floored. All that hard work? It was finally settling in.[iv,v] As of today, the number of streams continues to grow. My mixes and approach to putting together mixtapes were being well-received by people worldwide. It took me over a decade to achieve this. But even when I faced obstacles, negativity, and naysayers. I pushed through, blocked out the noise, and most importantly, never gave up. Even with the success I had achieved, I always remained true to the principles and values that had shaped my life. Never forgetting where I came from.

I devoted myself to making a positive impact on the lives of those around me. And I continued to work closely with unsigned artists, providing them with the support and guidance they needed to succeed.

Now, you might be wondering…

GROUP CHAT

But BAD, didn't you say you were also a producer? So when are you going to talk about that and the songs you've produced?

DJ BAD THA PROBLEM

I'm getting to that. Starting now…

Even though I was doing well as a DJ and A&R, I still had my eye on music production. That journey came with its own struggles. For as long as I can remember, I've dabbled in beat-making, producing, whatever you want to call it. I tried putting together a few beats here and there. Honestly, most of them were trash. And that's okay, everyone has to start somewhere.

The problem wasn't making the beats themselves. It was structuring and mixing them properly. That's where I really struggled. Eventually, I got the hang of beat structure. But mixing? I leave that to the professionals.

It took me eight years before I finally made a beat good enough for an artist to actually rap over. And I say "good enough" very lightly.

One day, my homeboy Spung hit me up after hearing one of my beats. He was working with an independent rapper from Alabama who went by the name of Da Big Dime. Dime heard the beat and wanted to use it. Of course, I said yes.

The track we made together was called "**Pavement**," featuring Pimp from *The Dirty Boys* and Prano Tha Don. Dime chose it as one of his official singles and even shot a music video for it.[vi]

The song ended up on his album *"**Da Alabama Animal.**"* When it dropped, "**Pavement**" became one of the most top streamed songs on the project. I was hyped at the time. But now, when I go back and listen to that beat… man, that beat was garbage.

I still love the song, but the beat? I have no clue why anyone would've wanted to rap over it. Some of the elements weren't synced with the tempo, the 808s were panned weird. It was just a mess.

But I don't blame anyone but myself. I had no clue how to mix back then. If I'd just sent the trackouts to a professional mixing engineer before handing it off to Dime, the beat could've sounded so much better.

Still, I'm grateful to Spung for the opportunity and to Da Big Dime for using my beat. You might think I gave up on producing after hearing how hard I was on myself. But I didn't. I kept practicing. Why? Because the more you practice, the better you get—and that's exactly what happened. Over time, I got good at it. There are other songs I've been involved with. Not as a beatmaker, but more so on the production side. But, I'll save those stories for another time.

My journey into music marked by the breaking of barriers and significant progress was however, far from complete. Each day brought new opportunities, new challenges, and additional reasons to keep pushing forward.

CHAPTER 5
BUILDING AN EMPIRE

Today, I'm living proof of what's possible when you stay hungry, focused, and never give up. Fueled by passion and strengthened by the enduring power of perseverance. My name is now becoming widely recognized due to my creative work with mixes, mashups, and mixtapes, along with my reputation for a strong work ethic that has significantly contributed to my success.

To prove it to you, allow me to break down what has happened these past four years. After more than a decade of consistently perfecting my craft, being persistent, and putting in work.

In 2021 during COVID, I got a phone call from my artist Poka Jones. He told me that some well-known figures in radio were putting together a virtual induction ceremony called the *National Black Radio Hall of Fame*. The event was being organized by the Atlanta Chapter, and they were looking for an editor and producer to put the show together.

Poka mentioned it was going to be showcased in front of hundreds of people, including the nominees who were some of the biggest names in radio. DJ Greg Street of V-103 Atlanta, Ryan Cameron of Magic 107.5 and 97.5, and Joe Madison of SiriusXM Urban View, just to name a few, would all be watching. Not gonna lie, I was a little nervous. I didn't want to screw up. But I stayed calm and thought, *No pressure.* With that being said, I accepted the opportunity.

He connected me with Mrs. Marsha, also known as the Radio Lady and the Vice President of the National Black Radio Hall Of Fame Atlanta Chapter. She told me what needed to be done, and I had only twenty-four hours to put it all together.

Long story short, the ceremony went great.[i]

Major thank you to Poka Jones for presenting me with the opportunity, and to Mrs. Marsha and the National Black Radio Hall Of Fame Atlanta Chapter for trusting me to get the job done.

In 2022, I had the opportunity to participate in a brief interview and live performance segment that led to me, City The Great, and ItsOnlyWrite being featured on *"Video Music Box,"* a well-known music television show.[ii] I owe a significant debt of gratitude to my boy City The Great, Ralph McDaniels, and the entire Video Music Box crew for their role in making this happen. Never in my life I thought I would be on TV. That moment was surreal.

During the summer of 2023, we had the distinct honor of performing live at the *Capital One Summer Stage Hip Hop 50th Anniversary Special Edition.* A memorable event held in Coney Island New York.[iii] In a momentous celebration of Hip-Hop's 50th anniversary, we were fortunate enough to share the stage with a remarkable group of legends, which included Special Ed, Kool Rock Ski, and a plethora of other influential figures in the Hip-Hop community.

In 2024, I was presented with a commemorative plaque in recognition of achieving the significant milestone of surpassing one million streams on the music streaming platform Audiomack.[iv] Not many independent artists can say they've achieved something this rare. Let alone receiving a plaque for it, but here we are. The impact of that plaque was far more profound than simply the numbers inscribed on it; it symbolized something much greater. It embodied all the work, the struggles, the triumphs and the countless hours spent toiling away over many years.

I had assumed that only those who had received a RIAA certification could obtain these kinds of plaques. Given their rarity and significance within the music industry. My initial understanding was far from accurate, as I subsequently learned that the reality of the situation was quite different.

Toward the end of the year, I received some unexpected news from a friend. My record label **CERTIFIED HITz Music Group**, had enjoyed a short-lived but nonetheless surprising promotional appearance on a billboard smack dab in the middle of Times Square!!ᵛ I was stunned! I still don't know who pulled the strings, but it happened. I even called my cousin that evening and asked him about it, but he claimed he knew nothing. So, I let it go.

As an entrepreneur, I'm always working on building my brand **CERTIFIED HITz Music Group**, producing mixtapes, beats, collaborating with artists, and helping the next generation of talent. That's what I do. My dedication to the craft and my commitment have cemented my place as a powerhouse in music.

It's been a long road full of ups and downs, but I kept going. From music production to my current role as a DJ to CEO, I've worn a lot of hats—but the passion's always stayed the same. Best believe, I am **not** gonna let anybody stop me or try to downplay what I've done. Call me a versatile problem!!

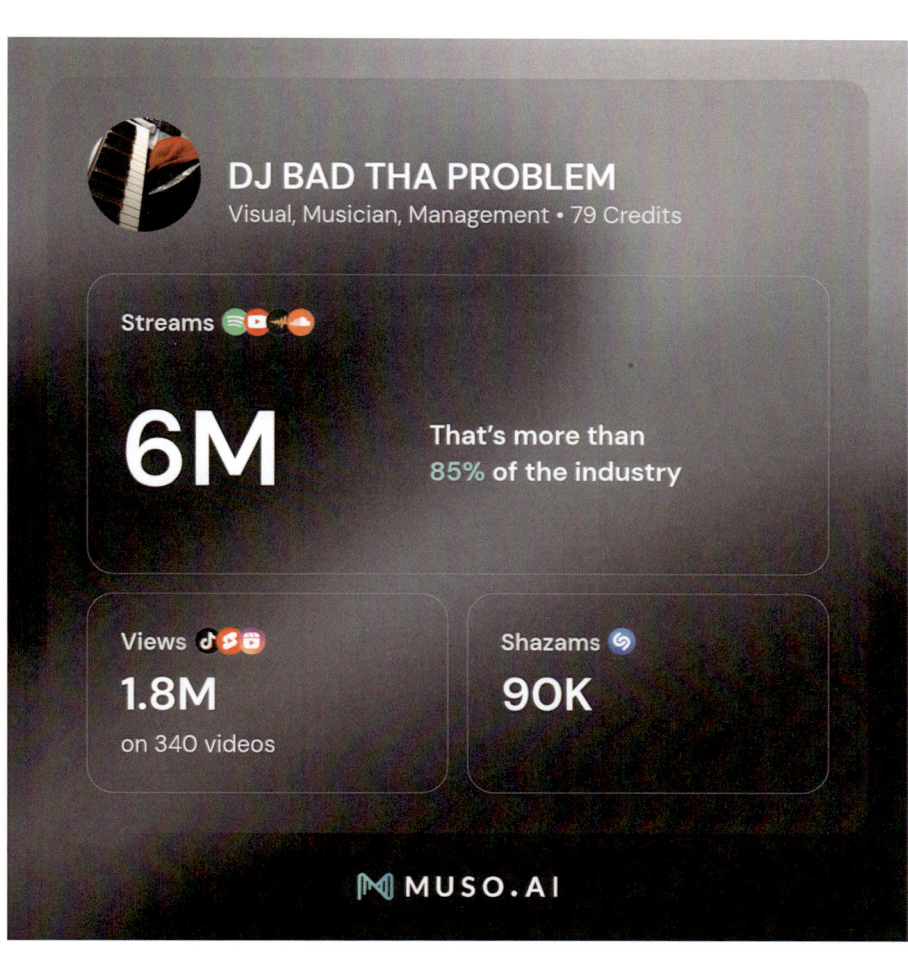

DJ BAD THA PROBLEM
Visual, Musician, Management • 79 Credits

Streams

6M

That's more than
85% of the industry

Views

1.8M
on 340 videos

Shazams

90K

DJ BAD THA PROBLEM
@dj-bad-tha-problem

ONE MILLION STREAMS

MUSO.AI

CERTIFIED HITz Music Group is in the Top 10% of Labels

Week of October 11 - 17, 2024

 imfreshdoe   🕐 11h

💙 118 likes

imfreshdoe S/o @mymixtapez @24kmixtapes @djbadthaproblem
@djkelo

Dj bad tha problem 🔍 +

⚙ Refine ▦ Sort ▾

All   Auction   Buy It Now

3 results

LOVE & R&B VOL 25 - R&B MIXTAPE- DJ BAD THA PROBLEM - 2015.

$3.79
+ $17.92

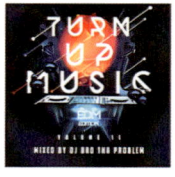

TURN UP MUSIC EDM EDITION - DJ BAD THA PROBLEM VOL 11 - 2015.

$4.17
+ $17.92

TURN UP MUSIC EDM EDITION - DJ BAD THA PROBLEM VOL 9 - 2015.

$4.17

AFTERWORD

Thank you for taking the time to read this short but meaningful memoir. I hope it inspires you to chase your dreams and never let anyone talk you out of them. As I mentioned in the **Preface**, there were people who didn't believe in me. But over time, those same doubters have come to regret it. Some even trying to find their way back into my life. They never saw the vision, and that's okay. I never expected them to.

What mattered was that I **never** gave up on myself, just like you should **never** give up on yourself. Every achievement I've reached took years of hard work and dedication.

If there's one lesson to take from this book, let it be this. Always strive for greatness, keep pushing forward, keep your foot on the gas, and the other on your hater's necks if necessary. Respectfully, of course.

> *The road to your dreams may be long, but every step forward is a step closer to the life you've imagined.*

ABOUT THE AUTHOR

DJ BAD THA PROBLEM is a professional DJ, as well as the Founder and CEO of the independent record label CERTIFIED HITz Music Group. In addition to BAD's roles as a producer and A&R, BAD has achieved significant success with mixtapes, which have garnered millions of streams.

DJ BAD has collaborated with numerous independent, major artists and brands. Additionally, BAD serves as the official DJ for City The Great and Southern Soul artist Poka Jones.

     facebook.com/djbadthaproblem
     x.com/djbadthaproblem
     instagram.com/djbadthaproblem
     youtube.com/@djbadthaproblem
     bsky.app/profile/djbadthaproblem.bsky.social

ACKNOWLEDGMENTS

I extend my heartfelt gratitude to my parents for their support and encouragement throughout the years. Them believing in me has been the cornerstone of my journey.

I am deeply grateful to my Team Titan DJ family for their camaraderie and support. A special thanks goes to DJ Kelo for his invaluable guidance and the opportunities he has generously given me over the years. Your mentorship has been important in my career.

I also want to express my sincere appreciation to DJ Pop Dukez for his continuous support and for opening doors that have significantly impacted my professional growth. Your contributions have been truly meaningful.

A special shout out to Johnathan, also known as GD, for your relentless promotion efforts on my behalf. The plaques you earned us through your hard work are still waiting for you, should you wish to claim them. We worked tirelessly together, and your work has not gone unnoticed.

Additionally, I owe a tremendous debt of gratitude to everyone who played a role in the massive marketing and promotion of my mixtapes. Though I cannot name you all individually, know that your efforts have been deeply appreciated.

I would like to acknowledge my artists, City The Great and Poka Jones. We have shared a long and rewarding journey, and I eagerly anticipate the future we will build together.

Our collective hard work is on the brink of bearing fruit, and I am grateful for your loyalty and commitment.

Finally, but by no means least, I extend my deepest thanks to all my supporters. Your continued faith and encouragement have been my driving force. Rest assured, the journey is far from over—there is much more to come.

THE KID AIN'T DONE YET!

– DJ BAD THA PROBLEM

For the skeptics, the curious, and the ones who want to walk in my footsteps. Review the next page. There you will see the certified proof behind the hustle.

NOTES

3. THE GRIND AND THE GLOW UP

i. DJ BAD THA PROBLEM's Turn Up Music [EDM Edition] mixtape series gaining traction on Audiomack. https://shorturl.at/D1D8J | https://shorturl.at/PP8Hu

ii. DJ BAD THA PROBLEM's mixtapes being sold on Ebay https://shorturl.at/WPP84 | https://shorturl.at/y3JsP

iii. DJ BAD THA PROBLEM's mixtapes being sold on various international websites https://shorturl.at/g2F5U | https://tinyurl.com/ydfvtyj4 | https://tinyurl.com/3yacds3x

4. BREAKING BARRIERS AND MAKING NOISE

i. Short Dawg shouts out DJ BAD THA PROBLEM & DJ Kelo on Instagram. March 2nd, 2015 https://tinyurl.com/4dnm4a72

ii. Fresh Muzik Vol. 2 hosted by Short Dawg | Mixed by DJ BAD THA PROBLEM & DJ Kelo. June 11, 2016 https://tinyurl.com/mwdcu4hm

iii. City The Great & Kool Rock Ski perform "Realigned" at the "2nd Annual Classic Hip Hop & R&B Cookout" https://tinyurl.com/5n8vk3fw

iv. DJ BAD THA PROBLEM receives over 1 million streams on Audiomack. See DJ BAD THA PROBLEM's Instagram post. September 24th, 2021 https://tinyurl.com/3n52mvcw

v. DJ BAD THA PROBLEM mixtape catalog exceeds over 4.1 million streams https://tinyurl.com/bdz34dmb

vi. Da Big Dime "Pavement" featuring Pimp from The Dirty Boys and Prano Tha Don. Produced by DJ BAD THA PROBLEM | https://tinyurl.com/3ajfycc9

5. BUILDING AN EMPIRE

i. National Black Radio Hall Of Fame Induction Ceremony 2020-2021 edited and produced by DJ BAD THA PROBLEM https://tinyurl.com/32frjrke

ii. DJ BAD THA PROBLEM & City The Great featured on Video Music Box https://tinyurl.com/d5xmet8y

iii. DJ BAD THA PROBLEM, City The Great, and ItsOnlyWrite perform at the Capital One Summerstage Hip Hop 50th Anniversary Special Edition in Coney Island, NY. https://tinyurl.com/bdeh9adz

iv. DJ BAD THA PROBLEM was presented with an Audiomack plaque for surpassing 1 million streams. For more details, see *24Hip-Hop*, January 31, 2024. https://tinyurl.com/2s49detk

v. CERTIFIED HITz Music Group featured on a billboard in Times Square, Manhattan, NY. https://tinyurl.com/yh2ap4as